Pathfinder 5

A CILT series for language teachers

On target

Teaching in the target language

Susan Halliwell
and
Barry Jones

Other titles in the PATHFINDER series:

Recording progress (John Thorogood)
Reading for pleasure in a foreign language (Ann Swarbrick)
Schemes of work (Laurie Kershook)
Communication re-activated: teaching pupils with learning difficulties
    (Bernardette Holmes)
Yes - but will they behave? Managing the interactive classroom
    (Susan Halliwell)

Acknowledgements

We could not have written this without the privileged experience of watching others learn to teach.

We are grateful to Caroline Mortlock for her cartoons.

First published 1991
Copyright © 1991 Centre for Information on Language Teaching and Research
ISBN 0 948003 54 5

Cover by Logos Design & Advertising
Printed in Great Britain by Direct Printers Ltd.

Published by Centre for Information on Language Teaching and Research, Regent's College, Inner Circle, Regent's Park, London NW1 4NS.

Contents

Introduction

We have set out to do three things in this book:

- to show how it is realistic and possible to teach in the target language;

- to propose effective strategies;

- to offer some suggestions for departmental workshops on the theme.

The *National Curriculum proposals* (DES/WO:1990:6) for modern foreign languages comment that:

Communicating in a foreign language must involve both teachers and pupils using the target language as the normal means of communication. Indeed this is essential if the objectives...are to be achieved. (para 3.18)

WHY?

There are three main ways in which it will help our learners if we teach them in the language they are learning.

- They need to experience the target language as a **real** means of communication.

- If we teach them in the language they are learning we give them a chance to develop their own in-built language learning system.

- By teaching through the target language we are bridging that otherwise wide gap between carefully controlled secure classroom practice and the unpredictability of real language encounters.

MAKING THE LANGUAGE REAL FOR THEM

It is not enough for us to keep pointing out to the learners that real people 'out there' actually use the target language both in daily speech and for normal understanding. Nor does it make much impact to say that at some later stage in their lives they themselves may really need to use it in both those ways. Both those concepts are too distant. We need to make the language real here and now. By teaching in the target language we can make it something that they themselves experience and use today. It is not just a vehicle for exercises and activities, to be put into real use sometime later.

HELPING THEM TO LEARN BY EXPERIENCING LANGUAGE AS WELL AS BY CONSCIOUS LEARNING

Until relatively recently, language classes have tended to operate almost exclusively as occasions for conscious learning. The focus has been on deliberately working things out as accurately as possible. But we all know that there is another way in which we can acquire a language. As part of our own language experience we have learnt a foreign language not only as a result of someone else's teaching but by finding ourselves in situations where it is being used around us. We get it by living it as well as by studying it. Our learners bring this same dual capacity with them to the foreign languages classroom. By teaching in the language we are giving this powerful system a chance of operating alongside deliberate language learning.

As they try to make sense of and find patterns in the language they encounter, they acquire language. It is, after all, this ability to apply in-built learning strategies which helps learners learn more than they are taught. It is certainly the case that they learn, too, in ways other than those which we decide for them.

BRIDGING THE GAP

In real life, speakers of a foreign language often have to cope with not understanding absolutely everything or with not being able to say exactly what they want. It will help our learners if right from the start we build up their confidence in this respect. They need to learn to take risks, both in understanding and in speaking. They need strategies for getting by. Teaching them in the target language prepares them for this.

1   What makes it possible to teach in the language they have not yet learned?

It is important to remember that messages are not carried by words alone.

Many teachers have one or more of the following reservations about teaching in the target language.

- They worry that children won't understand and won't know what to do.

- They worry that because classes resent being put in this position they will misbehave.

- They worry that they themselves sometimes do not know enough of the language to be able to do it effectively.

These worries arise because, as teachers whose work relies so heavily on words, we can easily forget two things. Firstly, nobody needs all the words they hear to understand perfectly what is said to them. Secondly, there are other sources of meaning. Even in our mother tongue a great deal of our understanding comes from our ability to interpret messages independently of the words. In fact, we often rely quite heavily on what we think the message is about rather than what is actually said. (This process is so common and so effective that most of the time we do not notice that we are doing it. In fact, it is most noticeable on the occasions when we get it wrong!)

We do not just take meaning **from** language; we also take meaning **to** language. There is a kind of reinforcing reciprocity.

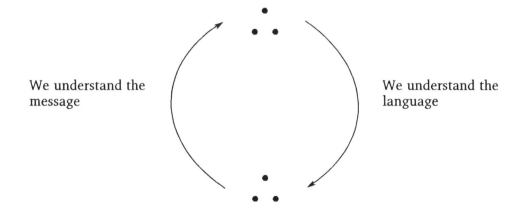

We understand the message

We understand the language

Among other things we take the message from:

★ the immediate context
★ our knowledge of how the world works
★ demonstrations
★ our reading of intonation patterns/facial expressions/general body language etc.

THE IMMEDIATE CONTEXT

Imagine you are standing watching someone you know doing some woodwork. They hold out their hand mumbling something through a mouthful of nails. You are unlikely to think that they are offering to shake hands. Even if we do not hear a word our understanding of the immediate context is likely to make us hand over a hammer.

KNOWLEDGE OF THE WORLD

We learn from experience to expect people to behave in certain ways in certain situations. In terms of the classroom that means that the learners have expectations about teacher behaviour. So, for example, if a teacher walks across to one of the class and hands over a pile of worksheets few children would think of asking what they have to do with them. They know. Indeed, these anticipated messages are sometimes so strong that the class ignores what you actually tell them to do and does what they expect you to want them to do! Even in the mother tongue the role of the language is often simply to confirm a message already received. In the case of a foreign language, the message we have already received will enable us to understand and to process the language that comes with it. For most schoolchildren this 'knowledge of the world' is still closely culturally determined. The more they encounter a foreign language in a cultural context the better they will interpret it when they meet it for real.

WATCHING FOR MEANING

Words on their own are a poor source of information. Imagine being instructed over the phone how to change a nappy. We are much more likely to be able to follow instructions if we can see someone doing what we have to do.

INTERPRETING SOCIAL SIGNALS

From our earliest days we read the messages from facial expression, gesture, body language and intonation. Irritation or encouragement, determination, enthusiasm and amusement do not need words.

Because the message is carried and interpreted through these and other channels, it means that in the classroom:

- the learners can understand what is going on even if they don't yet know the words/structures. (That is why it is possible to teach complete beginners in the language they are learning.)

- the teacher does not have to be a fluent bilingual, able to say anything and everything in the target language. Limited language can carry quite complex messages.

In fact, some people believe nonspecialists are often at an initial advantage over the native speaker. Although this may not be so, they are **trying** to do two crucial things:

- to go for clear messages in limited language, whereas the native speaker or highly skilled specialist tends to talk on, relying on words because for them they **do** carry the meaning. This is worth remembering if we are in the fortunate position of having an assistant in the school. Simplifying the language is something she or he will probably need particular help with.

- to provide a parallel source of information by means of actions, demonstrations, gestures, facial expressions, etc.

So we need to remember that we do **not** have to say everything in the target language which we would have said in English. In fact, if we do try to operate through the equivalent amount and the equivalent complexity in the target language, we can make life very difficult for the learners. They will then probably respond by making life difficult for us! Of course, as the classes get better at the language and get more used to the situation we can begin to rely on more words and to use more complex language. Meanwhile, to begin with we are trying to get the message across in two main ways in order to do three basic things:

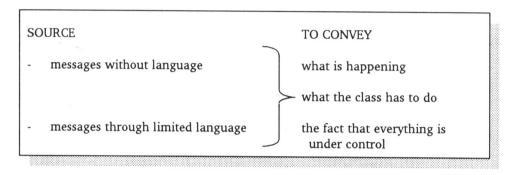

SOURCE	TO CONVEY
- messages without language	what is happening
	what the class has to do
- messages through limited language	the fact that everything is under control

Providing messages without language

Two key features help here:

- breaking things down into short easy stages;

- 'telling' by showing and doing.

These are in fact simply extending something we all do already in our teaching. If we watch good teachers teaching any subject in the mother tongue, they rarely describe a whole activity in one go and then expect the class to remember the whole thing. They are much more likely to set the activity up in stages. They also very often do what they are talking about as they talk about it. If we do this in a language class it is not just a longwinded way of going about it. In the process of setting the activity up by doing it we are:

- confirming the language patterns both for understanding and for the use that is about to follow;

- establishing more clearly than is possible with words alone, what the class has to do.

In the example that follows we have temporarily omitted any language other than the language being practised. This should illustrate how the message about what to do and how they should do it is carried by what the learners **see**.

TRUFFES AU CHOCOLAT

1 125 gr de cacao.

2 75 gr de beurre.

3 1 jaune d'oeuf.

4 ½ cuillerée de café soluble.

5 50 gr de granulés de chocolat.

6 2 cuillerées de sucre.

a Mélangez le cacao, le jaune d'oeuf, le café soluble, le beurre et le sucre.

b Roulez les truffes.

c Mettez les truffes dans des caissettes en papier.

d Mettez les truffes dans le frigo.

from *Attention* by Barry Jones, Cambridge University Press, 1987

It is quite common for textbooks or real first aid leaflets to describe ailments and injuries and their treatment by a series of numbered pictures. In the initial stages of teaching these we want the learners to recognise the sound of the phrases and mentally match them up with the event depicted. We can set up an activity to do this, entirely on the explain-by-showing-and-doing principle. If you were using an authentic leaflet the activity could go like this:

- hold up the leaflet and point to the appropriate page of the pictures (labelled a-j). Hold it so that the class can see whether they have found the right page on their photocopy

- write the numbers 1-10 on the board

- say aloud one of the phrases

- search **obviously** for the picture which matches the phrase

- write the letter of the matching picture alongside 1 on the board

- repeat the process for a second phrase. By the time you get to the third phrase the learners will be anticipating and will tell you which letter to write up

- pick up someone's exercise book and hold it up

- open it at the back

- while the class gets organised rub out the preliminary examples

- point to the numbers 1-10 and indicate that they should write out a similar list

- start again with a new phrase. (For the first two watch to see that they have got the idea and to confirm, for the slower ones, that they are on the right track. We can do this by again writing up the answers. After that we can leave them to it.)

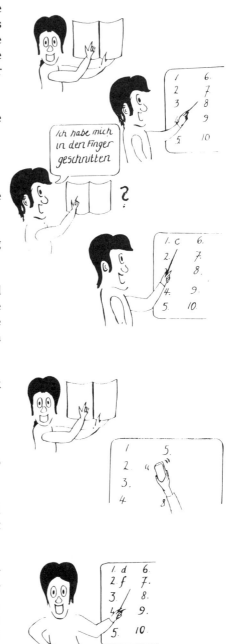

Written out like this it looks almost insultingly obvious. Yet it is precisely this kind of very simple system of non-verbal messages which enables us to teach even complete beginners in the language they are learning. Instead of trying to give all the information about the activity at the beginning, it has been built up stage by stage by actually doing it. At each stage the necessary information has been **seen**. This does not mean that the teacher is just relying on gesture and miming. The blackboard or OHP also acts as a very important source of visual information and instruction by example.

The same very simple process underlies all teaching in the target language. It is even **more** important, not less, when setting up more complicated activities and it remains crucial even when increasingly complex language is added.

By working in this way we are not just enabling our learners to cope with the target language. We are actively helping them to acquire it. A TV cookery demonstration is understandable with the sound switched off. Accompany it with language and as well as the cookery techniques the associated language is learned. We should not be too concerned that we do not know if **all** our learners in this situation are acquiring the **same** language, or, indeed, if they are acquiring **all** of it. What we can guarantee, however, is that, without it being systematically taught and practised, all of them will learn something that they would not otherwise have learned. In other words, learning can take place **without** explicit teaching.

We can now look at some strategies for adding limited language to the messages which are already carried by what the class can see and can predict.

Providing messages with limited language

It helps to:

- avoid long bursts of language without other sources of message;
- keep eye contact in silences and voice contact when looking away;
- use volume, intonation and emphasis to highlight meaning;
- use cognates initially where they exist;
- use marker words to convey the structure and a sense of purpose;
- signal the general nature of each activity;
- use single words to signal the specific nature of what you are about to say;
- use with a very small selection of all-purpose phrases;
- if English surfaces use it indirectly.

We will look at each of these separately and then see what they look like as a whole.

KEEPING IT SHORT

A long flow of the foreign language without any other source of message, particularly at the beginning of the lesson before the learners are tuned in, can produce panic and resentment. It helps to keep the message pithy and to use something else to back it up.

Example:

Instead of	Try
Aujourd'hui on va écouter une conversation entre Astérix et Obélix. Ils sont dans leur village en Bretagne. Bien! Je vais jouer la cassette. Puis vous allez répondre à mes 10 questions. Bien! Sortez vos cahiers et écoutez la cassette. Ça va?	1. *Regardez voilà Asterix voilà Obélix* (write names on OHP or board) 2. *Ils parlent.* (mime) 3. *Ils sont dans leur village.* (show) 4. *Voilà des questions sur la conversation.* (show on OHP) 5. *Écoutez la cassette.* (show, mime) 6. *Écrivez les responses dans votre cahier.* (pick one up) ...

KEEPING IN CONTACT

One of the problems of reducing the flow of language is that many of us have learned to express our classroom personalities through the style of our English. How does one convey the equivalent of *'Watch it!'* in French...? If language is limited, contact can seem limited for both parties. It is therefore all the more important that the teacher does not 'disappear'. If the class is feeling insecure it is more likely to switch off. We have got to signal somehow that we are still with them. After a while this will cease to be a problem. Once we and they are used to working in the target language our classroom personalities emerge as clearly as ever. Meanwhile however:

- when there has to be a silence, perhaps because we need to give them time to think ⟶ it is even more important that we look at individuals round the class;

- when we need to turn our attention away from them ⟶ it helps to use filler phrases to signal the pause is intended, e.g. *attendez une minute...* and/or to comment in the target language on what we are doing as we do it, e.g.

10

(drawing grid on the board) *bon voilà une ligne verticale... et puis encore une... voilà la troisième... et maintenant les horizontales... une... voilà... deux... et... trois... ça y est!*

PROVIDING STEPPING STONES

It will help the learners if we make key words stand out in some way. We can make them louder, more emphatic, or we can combine either of these with a pause. In this way we provide stepping stones of meaning through a flood of language. Equally importantly, by doing this we are also building up the learners' willingness and ability to predict and to work on the basis of partial understanding.

BUILDING ON WHAT THEY ALREADY KNOW

Sometimes there is a word which sounds sufficiently similar to the English to help understanding, especially if accompanied by confirming mime or gesture, e.g. *copiez... on change...* . Sometimes the cognate exists but would not be so readily used by a native speaker, e.g. *stop!...* In the latter case we can use the cognate initially and attach the less familiar word to it. Later, we can leave the new word to stand on its own, e.g. *Also, jetzt kopieren... nachschreiben... ja, nachschreiben... kopieren...* .

PROVIDING A CLEARLY STRUCTURED FRAMEWORK TO WHAT IS GOING ON

Little words like *jetzt, also, aber, inzwischen* in German and *d'abord, finalement, deuxième, maintenant, mais* in French, have the same effect as paragraphs have in writing. They show beginnings, endings, changes of focus, relationships between sections. They can signal that what is about to come is important. They say to the class *'come back in even if you switched off earlier'* or *'make sure you don't miss this bit.'* They refocus attention. They also give a comforting sense of shape and purposeful progress to the lesson.

SIGNALLING THE GENERAL NATURE OF THE ACTIVITY

Words like *écoutez, regardez, dessinez, travaillez avec un/e partenaire, test... aufpassen, hinsetzen, hinschreiben, Partnerarbeit*, etc provide something immediate and simple to respond to. They provide the first line security of knowing roughly what is going on. The more the learners understand what is going on, the less likely they are to look for an excuse to misbehave.

INDICATING THE NATURE OF THE LANGUAGE UTTERANCE THAT IS ABOUT TO COME

We often know what an utterance must be (e.g. question or answer) because we know what it means. But we have all seen classes sitting there wondering whether they have to repeat, answer or do something. So it will help them to know what sort of utterance is coming if we use cues like:

> *écoutez... question:...*
> *maintenant... exemple:...*

USING A SMALL SET OF KEY PHRASES

It is worth remembering how few phases we actually need. We are often very wordy in our mother tongue. Whereas in English we might say:

> '*Can you stop and listen, whether you have finished or not*', in French this can become simply, '*Bon, écoutez*'.

Or

> '*Now I want you to do this in pairs*' becomes '*Jetzt, Partnerarbeit*'

Or

> '*Let's have a bit of hush for a while, you lot*' shortens to '*Du calme!*'

Even more basically, *oui, non, mais, also bitte, na so was, faites comme ça, ne faites pas comme ça*, etc can be used for a whole variety of occasions including some of the less comfortable moments in a classroom.

Different intonation can also often extend the use of a single phrase. '*Was ist los?*' or '*Tu as un problème?*' can be genuine enquiries. They can also be a reproach or a reprimand. This use of intonation to extend the use of a limited range of language is something learners need to learn to do themselves in order to get by with limited language, so it is all to the good.

USING ENGLISH INDIRECTLY

There will inevitably be moments when English does arise naturally. Textbooks may have long passages of English by way of background or they may set exercises up in English. Without going into contortions, it is possible to use these but still to restrict the amount of English used. For example:

> *Regardez la page xx. Lisez l'anglais en silence...* (later) *Bon... question numéro 1.* (child answers in English) *Oui, il faut composter le billet...* etc.

There are also occasions when we will want to be absolutely sure that no one has the excuse later of claiming that they did not understand, for example in the setting of homework. Even this is not a problem in the target language once the class is used to the system. Meanwhile, as an interim measure we can use the board to provide a simultaneous parallel, e.g.

You say	**You write on the board**
Pour les devoirs ce soir:	homework!!!
lisez la page xx	page xx
regardez l'exemple B	e.g. B
choisissez le vocabulaire	some of the words in French
	↓
faites un poster	POSTER

Alternatively, one of the class can be used as a repeater station so that she or he has to summarise in English what has just been said. (This is interpreting for real, not just translating.) Finally, if single words in a text are proving a stumbling block there is no point being fanatical. After all, no one is asking you to spend half an hour trying to demonstrate the word hippopotamus or *'ensuite'*! Similarly, if a learner does not know a word in the target language, why should we object to something that comes out like *'Je n'ai pas de* felt tip'? A reply *'...Ah, tu n'as pas de stylo feutre'* combined with handing one over will supply both the missing word and the pen in a combination which is likely to be remembered.

However, we need to monitor this carefully. If we find ourselves supplying English words frequently, it is the beginning of the slippery slope to defeat. It does **not** help at any stage to:

★ keep asking if they understand
(They are not going to understand everything so they will play safe and say no. This is very defeating for both teacher and learner. In fact, they will nearly always have understood **enough** and we can **see** if they understand by the way they react.)

★ check constantly for exact meaning and translations
(Again this implies that they have not understood unless they can reproduce it exactly in the mother tongue. We know from our own experiences that there are occasions when we have understood but cannot find the exact mother tongue words.)

★ keep switching in and out of the target language
(If we do this we easily destroy both the urge and the opportunity to deal with the foreign language. Learners will simply operate with the English.)

Here are two examples of all these ideas put together. The first example suggests what could be done to set up a pairwork activity using the textbook. This assumes there has already been a lively introduction, using mime, objects and actions, to provide a clear explanation of the appropriate language below:

A	B

une coupure
  (pas trop grave)
	lavez la blessure avec du coton
	passez une pommade antiseptique
	couvrez avec un pansement, ou un
	    sparadrap

un bleu	*trempez du coton dans de l'eau* *froide et propre* *mettez un pansement*
un mal de tête	*trouvez des cachets d'aspirine* *lisez l'étiquette* *donnez la dose correcte*
une brûlure *(pas trop grave)*	*mettez de l'eau très froide* *séchez avec soin* *couvrez avec un pansement sec*
une piqûre d'insecte	*mettez de l'eau froide* *passez une pommade antiseptique*

Now we want to set up the pairwork.

4 Etes-vous secouriste?

Travaillez avec un partenaire.
Votre partenaire couvre la colonne
A. Vous couvrez la colonne B.

Vous dites:
Pour une coupure?
A tour de rôle!

Votre partenaire dit:
lavez la blessure
passez une pommade
couvrez avec un pansement etc

Colonne A	Colonne B
une coupure	
un bleu	
un mal de tête	
une brûlure	
une piqûre d'insecte	

from *Jeux de mots* by Barry Jones, Cambridge University Press, 1987

Words	Actions
1. *Maintenant... regardez...*	1. Hold up your book.
2. *A la page 16*	2. Open your own book at 16 and turn it so they can all see the page.
3. *Exemple*	3. (You could write e.g. on the board to emphasise the cue.)
(4. *Attention, John*)	4. Walk over to John. Make sure he has the right page open. Point to the section on the page you are about to use.
5. *Un/e volontaire, s'il vous plaît...*	5. (This is a cognate in French which works.)
6. *Merci. Viens ici*	6. Beckon the volunteer to the front.
7. *Moi, je couvre la colonne B*	7. Cover column B in your book with your hand. Show your volunteer what you have done and then show the class.
8. *Toi, mon partenaire, tu couvres la colonne A*	8. Point to the learner's book column A and mime covering it over.
9. *La classe, regardez bien... Une démonstration!*	9. (Write the word 'demonstration' on the blackboard.) Look round and make sure everyone is watching.
10. *Tu commences...* (whisper... *pour une coupure:*)	10. Point to your partner to begin. Prompt with a stage whisper if required.
11. (learner). *Pour une coupure?*	11. Your volunteer partner speaks.
12. (teacher again)... *Alors... pour une coupure ...lavez la blessure avec du coton...*	12. Make it obvious that you are looking for the reply from the list in the book and hold the book up to show where you have found it.

You will probably need to do two more examples before... '*à vous maintenant!...*'

Example 2 follows the same techniques, this time for a free standing activity. Each pair of learners has an envelope containing sets of cards. One set has pictures of people. The other set has matching descriptions.

Words	Actions
1. *Regardez*	1. Hold up the envelope containing the cards.
2. *Voilà des cartes*	2. Take out the cards.
3. *Il y en a deux sortes*	3. Hold up one pile in each hand.
4. *Voilà des images...*	4. Show the pile of picture cards.
5. *...et voilà des phrases*	5. Show sentence cards.
6. (Time for a *'Faites attention'* here so they know it is the big moment of the explanation?!) *Mettez les images comme ça...*	6. Show picture cards again and put them face down in a pile (worth repeating the action to stress that they should be face down).
7. *... et les phrases comme ça.* (Counting as you do it usefully fills in the silence while completing the action.)	7. Deal out sentence cards into three rows of four, face down.
8. *Je prends une carte... Ah, c'est une fille qui porte...*	8. Take the top card from the picture pile, and comment on it.
9. *... Je cherche... je choisis ...voilà!*	9. Choose (with a touch of drama) a picture card from the spread.
10. *Elle porte un pantalon rouge.*	10. Hold up the sentence card (word side towards the class) and read it.
11. *C'est vrai - elle porte un pantalon? Oui. Rouge? Non. Alors, ce n'est pas vrai.*	11. Hold the two up together, repeating the phrase, looking backwards and forwards from one to the other.
12. *Alors je remets l'image SOUS les autres cartes...*	12. Replace the picture card UNDER the pile, making sure that UNDER is clear.
13. *...et puis je remets la phrase.*	13. Replace the sentence card in its original position.

from an article (under S Halliwell's former name of S Maclennan) in NALA Journal 18, July 1987

If we start with a skeletal framework of simple language like this, then we can easily fill it out as their (and our!) confidence and competence grows. For example:

| JETZT | ································· | PARTNERARBEIT |

can soon become

Also JETZT *machen wir was anderes. Nun sollt ihr das mit euren*

PARTNERN *üben.*

This question of our confidence in the approach is crucial. **There is nothing inherently difficult in teaching in the target language.** However, if either the teacher or the class are not used to it, it is the changeover which is difficult. We need strategies for carrying us through the temporary insecurities of change. This brings us to the second section.

2   Strategies for implementation

We offer these ideas under three headings:

- strategies for the teacher
- strategies for the learners
- strategies for the department as a whole

For the individual teacher

We each have a choice between:

either	the *'slowly slowly'* approach
or	the *'it's now or never'* approach

If you prefer the 'slowly slowly' approach we suggest you:

★ Build up a repertoire of words and phrases. You could use the following headings as a guideline.

INSTRUCTIONS FOR CLASSROOM ACTIVITIES, e.g.

- *Bon, écoutez!*
- *Regardez!*
- *Trouvez la page xx*
- *Répétez!*
- *Lisez...*
- *Ecrivez...*
- *Dessinez...*
- *Couvrez...*
- *Collez...*
- *Choisissez...*
- *Faites l'exercice (b), à la page xx*

- *Faites un poster...*
- *Mimez...*
- *Copiez...*
- *Jouez...*
- *Parlez plus fort/moins fort/plus vite/moins vite*
- *Remplissez la grille!*
- *Cochez votre grille!*
- *Vrai ou faux?*
- *Testez votre mémoire!*

INSTRUCTIONS FOR CLASSROOM ORGANISATION, e.g.

- *(Travaillez) avec un/une partenaire*
- *(Travaillez) en groupes de quatre*
- *A tour de rôle*
- *A vous maintenant*

- *Echangez votre cahier...*
- *Corrigez...*
- *Asseyez-vous! Assieds-toi!*
- *Dépêchez-vous! Dépêche-toi!*

CHANGE OF ACTIVITY 'MARKERS', e.g.

- *d'abord...*
- *maintenant*

- *alors,...*
- *pour terminer...*

NATURE OF ACTIVITY 'MARKERS', e.g.

- *question:*
- *exemple:*
- *réponse:*

MILD DISCIPLINE EXHORTATIONS, e.g.

- *du calme, s'il vous plait*
- *silence!* (said **softly**)
- *ne fais/faites pas ça!*

- *faites comme ça*
- *tu as un problème?*

(Beyond a certain point, however, these may not be effective. On occasions, it will make sense to suspend the language lesson and deal with the matter unequivocally in English.)

EXPRESSING EMOTIONAL REACTIONS, e.g.

- *Bravo!*
- *(Très) bien* (as a reaction to the message and **not** to the grammatical accuracy!)
- *Bien dit!*
- *Bien écrit!*
- *Bof...*
- *Je n'aime pas ça!*
- *Excellent!*
- *Affreux!* (but avoid these applying to grammatical accuracy; they should be a response to the **content/message**)
- *Parfait!*
- *Tu crois?* (example: learner says: *Il fait beau aujourd'hui,* you say: *Tu crois?*)
- *Génial!*

★ Experiment with distinct blocks of target language talk in a lesson rather than constantly switching between languages. This can be backed up by:

● asking the learners to share the experimental nature of the enterprise.

('*See how long we can keep going in Spanish'. 'I am going to do this bit all in Russian. If you get stuck keep going and we will sort it out later'*).

20

- explicitly practising phrases with them as a warm-up to a block of target language teaching.

It is only fair to point out that there can be a very real problem with the 'slowly slowly' approach. It is rather like doing income tax returns. There is always a very good reason for not doing it today:

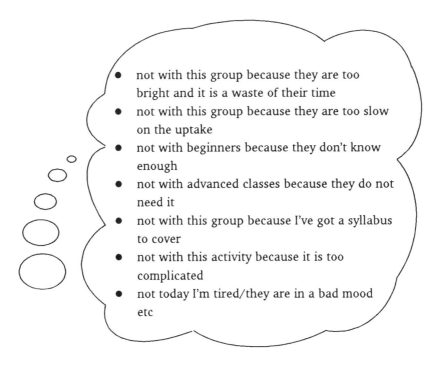

- not with this group because they are too bright and it is a waste of their time
- not with this group because they are too slow on the uptake
- not with beginners because they don't know enough
- not with advanced classes because they do not need it
- not with this group because I've got a syllabus to cover
- not with this activity because it is too complicated
- not today I'm tired/they are in a bad mood etc

There is even the self-reinforcing:

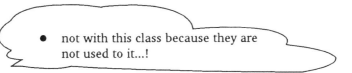

- not with this class because they are not used to it...!

The danger here is that if we do not develop the strategies for the elements we find difficult we will never do it. However, it is possible to combine some of the advantages of the two approaches. For example, it is feasible and sometimes more reassuring to:

- try it out with just one class first. Choose the class you feel most comfortable with. **But with that one class go all out.**

- start with the next new intake and build target language use up through the school as those classes move up through it. In that sense it is 'slowly slowly'. But again with those classes **go all out.**

Finally, there is the question of grammar.

Here it may help in deciding what to do, if we distinguish three main ways of teaching grammar. They are not mutually exclusive. Most of us use one or more of them. However, they each make slightly different demands on our use of the target language. By identifying which approach we are employing we can then identify the most sensible target language strategy for that approach. For example:

Approach 1   Letting the grammar emerge implicitly through the work. ——➤ In this case we simply teach in the target language as suggested in earlier sections of this book.

Approach 2   Making the grammatical patterns visually and aurally explicit.——➤ In this case the board or the OHP is used to set out the pattern using different shapes, colours, blutak-ed endings etc. Even something as simple as grouping vocabulary or structures as we write them up can help. We can then use the target language to draw attention to the visual pattern with additional key phrases like: *regardez la différence... ça change c'est important... Problem... passt auf... nicht vergessen,* etc.

Approach 3   Discussing the grammar explicitly in grammatical terminology.——➤ In this case we can either teach limited terminology in the target language and use that, and/or we can provide consolidating blocks of grammar work in English which are kept clearly separate from the rest of the work, either at ends or beginnings of lessons.

For the learners

If the learners are to be encouraged to use the target language in return then there will have to be ways of providing them with what they need. This has got to be quite deliberate because classroom pupil language does not usually surface either in the textbooks or in what we say as we are teaching. For example they will need phrases in the target language for:

talking to you, e.g.

j'ai fini

je ne comprends pas

monsieur!
mademoiselle!
répétez s'il vous plaît
encore une fois s'il vous plaît
je n'ai pas de...
je ne peux pas voir
pardon
chouette (as they receive a good mark for homework!)

talking to each other, e.g.

non tu commences

vite

non c'est à toi

copie
mets
écris
répète
encore une fois s'il te plaît
ne fais pas ça
donne moi...
ça marche
c'est génial
c'est ennuyeux
ça y est

Just giving them a list to learn is unlikely to encourage them or to prove to be an easy task. Here are some other suggestions:

- As events occur in class (such as people absent when you take the register, hands up to leave the room, or a late entry), supply the target language phrase for what is needed. For example:
    Er ist nicht hier. Er ist krank.
    Puis-je quitter la salle?
    Perdone me por llegar tarde.

- Similarly, give the learners in the target language the words that they have just used to show pleasure or an emotional reaction.

- During the lesson, as these words and phrases occur write them on the board in a list to one side. (It helps to have a 'scribble patch' where you can write 'extras' like this without getting in the way of the main work you are doing.) The words are then there as a reminder during the lesson and as the basis for a useful filler at the end of the lesson if you have a few minutes to spare.

- Later, write these words and phrases on card. You can do this yourself or, better still, get some of the class to do so, perhaps in large print on the word processor in the IT lesson. Pin the cards around the room (or even on the ceiling!). When needed they are then always there for reference.

- Introduce a new phrase and challenge the class to see how many times they can use it appropriately in the lesson. You can keep a running score in the scribble patch.

- Before setting up group or pairwork, deliberately practise some of the phrases they can use while they are doing the activity, e.g. *'Moment bitte!'* *'Nicht kucken!' 'Los!'* Introduce one or two new ones and remind them of some they have already met. As well as practising how to say them, you can leave them up on the board or OHP as a prompt if required.

For the department

Whichever approach a teacher chooses, it is difficult making changes like this alone. It is much more helpful to have a policy for the whole department. Then the learners do not think they have the misfortune to have a teacher who sets out to make their life awkward. Teachers can also compare notes and support each other in the experiment. Here are some suggestions for departmental strategies:

- Have a departmental policy and keep to it.

- Work out an agreed starter list of language like the examples on p 23.

- If possible, go into each others' classrooms. Firstly, it is often much easier to see from the back of the room what could have been done. Secondly, someone else notices the slippages that we ourselves miss when we are in full flow. Thirdly, there is nothing quite like having a colleague in the room to encourage one to make a success of something and really try!

- Decide as a department how to share with the learners what you are doing, what it involves for them and how it will help them.

- Decide as a department how to convey to the parents the 'new' approach and the thinking behind it. For example, some departments run demonstration events with the parents themselves as the class so that they can get the feel of what is involved.

- Hold some departmental workshops on INSET days.

The final section offers some ideas for these workshops.

3   Ideas for departmental workshops

The activities suggested here are intended as starting points and as a stimulus to developing ideas which suit the needs of your particular department. Most of them can be practised 'for real' on your own in the course of your daily teaching. However, practising teaching ideas on and with a small group of our colleagues has all kinds of advantages when we are working out a new approach or improving existing techniques. Precisely because the event is not 'for real', we have the freedom to experiment and take risks without matters getting out of hand. We can laugh together over the things which do not quite work. We can stop and start again. We can produce an immediate revised version while the first attempt is still fresh in our minds. What is more, we have the advantage of having other people there who know what we are trying to do and can therefore give us explicit feedback of a kind which is missing from the classroom. We can also see in what others do a reflection of some of the things we ourselves do, both their advantages and disadvantages. We benefit from the additional ideas of other members of the department who may suggest things or spot problems we would never have thought of on our own. In turn, we can find ourselves stimulated to new ideas by what the others do. All too often we have little opportunity to learn from and with each other in this way once we leave our initial training. The ideas which follow offer a chance to do just that. They focus in different ways on:

- making the most of the non-language messages
- learning to keep the language simple
- setting up work in stages by showing and doing

Suggestion 1   TO PRACTISE CONVEYING SIMPLE CLASSROOM
INSTRUCTIONS BY GESTURE AND EXAMPLE

You could:
- each write on strips of paper several of the instructions you would expect to have to issue in a language class. Put all of the strips into a bag or box. Take it in turns to pick out a strip 'blind' and **without saying anything at all** 'instruct' the others in the group to do it.

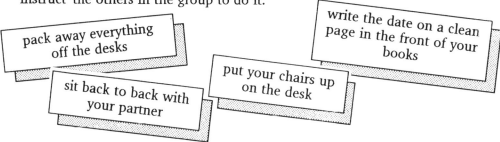

Suggestion 2 TO PRACTISE GIVING MORE COMPLEX INSTRUCTIONS IN THE SAME WAY BUT STAGE BY STAGE

You could:
- use strips of paper as before to collect a selection of the kind of more complicated instructions you may have to give when setting up pairwork or group work. Again, take it in turns to instruct the others **without at this stage using any words**. On this occasion concentrate on breaking down the instructions into stages.

'A's get up and move round to stand in front of 'B's facing them across the desk

group yourselves in fours round one desk/table each with a textbook propped up in front of you so that the others can't see what you are doing

Suggestion 3 TO PRACTISE SHOWING HOW TO DO SOMETHING

You could:
- each choose in advance something which you can teach the others to make e.g. a paper model or a chocolate truffle. Show them how to do it stage by stage, still **without saying anything**.

Suggestion 4 TO IDENTIFY A CORE OF SIMPLE PHRASES AND WORDS

You could:
- collect and share a basic list of marker phrases, signal words, cues and all-purpose phrases you are likely to need (see p 23 for some guideline headings). If there is an assistant in school they will be invaluable here. They too will benefit from thinking of the **simplest** version.

Suggestion 5 TO IDENTIFY A SIMPLE CORE OF WORDS FOR THE
LEARNERS

You could:
● agree on the content of, and each design, an initial *'pour vous aider'* board,
wall posters or 'inspiration clouds' which the learners consult when in
difficulty.

Suggestion 6 TO PRACTISE KEEPING LANGUAGE SIMPLE

You could:
● agree to restrict yourselves to a **limited** number of phrases (e.g. *écoutez, regardez, faites comme ça* + a free choice of three more) and use those few phrases to back up the kind of demonstration as indicated under Suggestion 4, e.g. teach the others how to make a fortune teller.

Suggestion 7 ANOTHER ACTIVITY TO PRACTISE KEEPING LANGUAGE SIMPLE

You could:
● each choose a language of which you know only very little or get someone else in the department to teach you a limited number of phrases as in Suggestion 5. Then take it in turns to use mime, gesture, drawing, OHP and example backed by those few phrases to set up one of the previous activities.

Suggestion 8 TO IDENTIFY AND EXTEND THE RANGE OF POSSIBLE WAYS OF 'TELLING' BY SHOWING

You could:
● choose an activity which is common to all of you and take it in turns to set the activity up using a different method of showing, e.g.

one concentrates on using the OHP
one uses flashcards (words or pictures)
one uses only the blackboard
one uses real objects
one uses only the book or leaflet itself

Compare the effect of each of these and discuss ways of combining them.

Suggestion 9 TO PRACTISE SETTING ACTIVITIES UP STAGE BY STAGE

You could:
● make a list of some of the activities most common in your teaching materials, e.g. introducing a tape listening comprehension, setting up paired dialogue from picture prompts, launching a class *'sondage'*, playing a memory game, written exercises. Take it in turns to set up one of them using all the techniques of 'telling by showing', and limited phrases. This time concentrate on setting the event by **doing** each stage **with** the 'class'.

Suggestion 10 TO COMPARE THE ADVANTAGES OF DIFFERENT WAYS OF INTRODUCING ACTIVITIES

You could:
- agree on one common but fairly complex activity you are all likely to introduce at some stage, e.g. 'battleships' or a class survey grid. In advance, each prepare independently a way of explaining by showing and doing in stages and compare the effectiveness of the different approaches in conveying the meaning alongside the language. Try to draw out any generalisable principles.

Suggestion 11 TO PRACTISE HIGHLIGHTING GRAMMAR PATTERN VISUALLY

You could:
- each choose in advance a particular grammar pattern, e.g. the relative clause in German, the preterite in Spanish, the partitive in French, and take it in turns to build that pattern up on the board and OHP using a few general target language comments to highlight the crucial points (see p 22). If you can do this in a language that some of your colleagues do not share, then all to the good.

Suggestion 12 TO PRACTISE DISCUSSING GRAMMAR IN THE TARGET LANGUAGE

You could:
- jointly make a list of a few key grammatical terms in the target language and then repeat Suggestion 11 with these few terms added.

Suggestion 13 TO PRACTISE MAKING UNAVOIDABLE ENGLISH AS INDIRECT AS POSSIBLE

You could:
- each choose a page from your textbook that uses a great deal of English (for example background information or comprehension questions in English) and briefly practise keeping your own target language going, even if the 'class' are temporarily having to work in English (see example p 13).

Suggestion 14 TO PRACTISE THE USE OF PARALLEL ENGLISH AS AN EFFECTIVE INTERIM DEVICE

You could:
- briefly take it in turns to set 'homework' or convey other detailed crucial information using the board to provide summarised information in English as you talk in the target language.

SOME GENERAL POINTS

- If you can, bring in a native speaker to help with these activities. This helps the department linguistically, gives the assistant the boost of a key role to play and, equally importantly, shows the assistant(e) strategies she or he will need for teaching in the native tongue.

- If you have a departmental video camera, why not video yourselves doing some of these activities?

- See if you can persuade some colleagues from other subject departments to join you to provide a 'class'. If they don't speak very much of the target language all the better. In fact, we should also not forget that our science colleagues in particular are very familiar with the ideas and techniques of explaining by showing and will have ideas to offer.

- If you are a very small department some of the ideas as they appear above would be difficult to set up. Schools often have their INSET days on the same day. If you cannot find colleagues from other subjects willing to act as guinea pigs why not see if you could join forces with language colleagues from another school for the day?

- If you have recent entrants to the profession in the department, or PGCE students placed in the school on teaching practice, it will be worth asking them for ideas, examples and demonstrations. Most of them will have been encouraged to teach in the target language from the start. It will also help them to discover that they have expertise to offer as well as so much to learn.

TROUBLESHOOTING

Yes, but what if...

★ ...they reply in English to what we say in the target language.

This can happen for several reasons:

a. they may want to annoy or provoke or try to be awkward by not 'playing the game'. If so, it is probably best to ignore their reaction and continue, in a simple version of the target language.

b. they can be genuinely lost. If this happens, rephrase what you have just been saying in the target language, e.g.

you: *Jetzt macht ihr das mit eurem Partner oder mit eurer Partnerin, bis einer von euch gewonnen hat. Und dann umtauschen!*

them: You mean we swap over...

you: *Ja! Wenn einer gewonnen hat, tauscht ihr um.* (+ mime)

Or failing this you can ask one member of the group to be *Dolmetscher/ interprète.*

'Peter. Sag das bitte auf Englisch.'

At least here you stay in the foreign language, whilst someone else's English reassures or clarifies.

c. they are being lazy. You know your class. This might be a moment to insist.

★ ...they produce a mixture of the target language and English.

If they are willing to do this we are more than half way there, so continue to react as if it had all been in the foreign language. If you believe the English was only a momentary substitute for a lost or forgotten word or phrase, supply this as part of a natural response in the foreign language.

★ ...they make mistakes.

They are bound to make mistakes and need to do so, if what they are doing is concentrating on conveying meaning, rather than being over-concerned with correct linguistic form. Again, in as natural a way as possible, rephrase their statement or response in an appropriately correct version of their original.

★ ...they talk to each other in English.

Sometimes this is inevitable. However, it is always worth asking ourselves whether we have taught them the target language versions of what they come out with in English. If not, then the responsibility lies with us and not with them! If the reason seems to be a lack of motivation or willingness, try appointing one of the pupils in a partner activity as *'le juge linguistique'* who says *'Répète en Français, s'il te plaît'/'Sag das bitte auf Deutsch'*, or who, in a class activity, says (using one of a set of agreed formulae), *'C'est quoi en français?'... 'Wie sagt man das auf Deutsch?'*

★ **...you are in the middle of explaining and they become impatient and say 'What's all that in English?'**

Try to: add as many helpful visual explanations of the language as possible (using coloured pens, chalks, different shapes, letters on card blutak-ed to the board.)

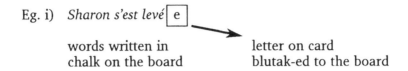

Eg. i)   *Sharon s'est levé* e

words written in   letter on card
chalk on the board   blutak-ed to the board

Then (after, in this example, changing the name before the verb) ask one of the class to come out and select the correct letter from a pile on the teacher's table.

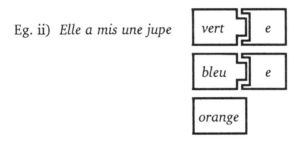

Eg. ii) *Elle a mis une jupe*   *vert*   *e*

bleu   *e*

orange

Again, ask members of the class to come out and make up their jig-saw pieces into, say, appropriate captions for a series of magazine photos.

If all else fails... encourage an interpreter to explain in English the pattern which you have been trying to illustrate. Sometimes an individual's version of what's going on can be clearer than anything that you have said in any language!

★ **...you have made a mistake.**

Say: *Zut! C'est **un** parapluie -*
J'écris ça pour vous aider: un parpluie.
(cover 'un') Toi- Georges, répète!...
*Georges- **un** parapluie.*
Toi- Georges est très intelligent, n'est-ce pas?

★ **...they want to interrupt and translate.**

Say:　　'*Oui, c'est bien ça*' if they are correct.
　　　　'*Non, c'est faux*' if they are incorrect.

Then give an appropriately rephrased version of what you were saying in the foreign language.

★ **...you could save an awful lot of time by saying something in English.**

Do so, if it is only one word. (Think how many times you do this in the foreign language when speaking English to a French or German native speaker.) Better to sustain your message with one word whispered in English than to spend five minutes swinging from the chandeliers trying to mime '*faire la culbute*' (to somersault).

If, however, you 'give in' for anything longer or more complex, then you are doing your class and yourself a disservice.

Perhaps you have not been:

a. simplifying sufficiently;

b. backing up your oral instructions or explanations with numbered and staged instructions in the target language, written on the board as you speak;

c. using key words on the board which have English equivalent look-alikes or quick sketches to exemplify meaning.

★ **...you have a new child in the class who does not understand.**

a. Use the interpreter technique with someone from the class who has befriended the newcomer.

b. See if any of the class can explain something in the target language.

c. Spend time during the lesson, when the class is doing something independently of you, explaining how you give explanations or set activities in the target language, and what sort of language you use to do this. If you have already written many of these on cards displayed around the room, ask one of the class to explain what is there.

★ **...they just dismiss the whole process as stupid.**

Do not give up! Try a timed *'x minutes en français', 'x Minuten auf Deutsch'!* on the next occasion you see them.
Set yourself, and them, limited targets.
Congratulate them afterwards! *'Bien! 10 minutes en français'* - *'Schön, 10 Minuten auf Deutsch! Prima!'*
See if, next lesson, they can beat their record.

Final comment

Finally, in practising these approaches we must not lose sight of why we are doing it, or they just become inflexible and even burdensome rituals. This brings us back to the starting point of the book.

We are teaching in the target language in order to give our learners a better chance of learning another language effectively. We are:

- making the language a real tool that they experience in use;

- giving them the confidence to get by when they emerge from the protection of the classroom;

- above all we are providing another very powerful channel of learning the language itself.